Things to Make

Dona Herweck Rice

I like making things with my hands. Sometimes I get messy, but I have fun.

Other people like to make things, too. In this book, some of them will tell you about what they make.

I am making a rug in the old way.

The stuff to make the rug comes from a desert plant. I find what I need. Then I go to work.

5

I am making a quilt.

No other quilt looks
like mine. I take my time
so it comes out right.

My mother showed me
how to make blankets.
Her mother showed her.

Now I teach my children
how it is done.

I make baskets like my
people did many years ago.

My baskets will last a long time. I am proud of them.

Long ago, my people
made pots from clay.
The pots had many uses.

Today I make pots just like they did.

I baked my first cake
when I was a little girl.

Now I am a pastry
chef. I make desserts
with my own hands.

I love to make things with my hands. There is only one other thing I like as much. It is teaching others what I know.